THE QUARANTINE COLLECTION

The Quarantine Collection

Looking for a light, in the dark

T. M. WOODWORTH

T. M. Woodworth

The Quarantine Collection

Looking for Light, in the Dark

By: T. M. Woodworth

ACKNOWLEDGMENTS

For AJ, TC, CM for your tireless patience and support of my art and being the inspiration behind so much of the writing and the living. You have my whole heart.

To Toni, who is bright and brilliant and was my tour guide through the storm showing me how to love and let go.

To my dearest friend and editor, Shannon. Thank you for helping me find dreams I didn't realize I had and tolerating all the things writers and authors ask of our friends.

To Saba, who let me learn from her and let my love for Raya grow with hers. Who let me write her story.

To Nola, who made me laugh again. Who reminded me why and how I became who I am. And showing us all how to un-apologetically love ourselves. Boom!

To SuzyQ, for being the best international criminal I know! And the only one who knows Omaha and Vancouver!

To Kristan, who read many iterations of this with love and time. And reminded me to get some exercise!

To Barb and her late, dear Mother, who we lost during Covid. The woman who made her the loving, fierce, beautiful friend she is.

To Annie, who cheered for us all and made room in her fabric for our family.

To Laura, who taught me how a good walk, with a good friend, could heal anything.

To Sarah McKinstry Brown, for being my inspiration always and my favorite writer and poet.

To my Mom, for getting vaccinated and always encouraging me to write!

To my two best brothers for loading a UHaul, for listening to my writings as I wrote them, for loving each other enough to jump in the pool with one another when we're drowning, and for always being my ride or dies.

A MULTIMEDIA EXPERIENCE - IF YOU WANT IT TO BE

If you are still a dedicated and focused reader in the year 2023, I commend you for your self control and attention span! For me, reading gets harder and harder as a singularly focused endeavor. As we are inundated with messages and notifications and being accessible to everyone 24/7, the ability to sit down, read and tune out the 'noise,' I find more and more challenging.

With that in mind, I have created a playlist of songs to play and listen to, while you read each chapter. The songs epitomize the tone, the mood and the content in many ways and create a 'multimedia experience' to allow you space and time to read, perhaps with your earbuds in, perhaps with breaks in between each chapter to dance in the kitchen to a song you particularly like and then return to the next section.

I hope it allows you to be stimulated in the ways we have all gotten used to - sight, sounds, thoughts - all at once and to relive what we all lived through. Together.

To receive a link to the playlist, email:
TMWoodworth313@gmail.com

This is the story of a family's migration from America to Canada - searching for opportunity and safety from gun violence, white nationalism, governmental corruption and online radicalization that has gripped their country. Just 15 months after they arrive, the COVID-19 pandemic hits and deepens their resolve to protect their family, their anguish in coming to terms with this new world as global politics shift as they try to raise their children in a new world full of new challenges, new darkness and new beginnings. This story captures the historical moments of the times we lived through and makes permanent the record of what happened.

The same people who told us, "It could never happen here." And later, "It won't be that bad" will now try to tell us these years, "weren't that bad." That would be a lie. 2016-2020 were some of the most difficult years to be an American, to live in America and it was difficult globally, for all of humanity as authoritarianism was on the rise across the globe. For those of us living in Western Democracies we felt the pain, the fear, the anxiety and the responsibility to fix it, in a palpable way. We must never forget just how bad it was; just how closely Democracy, as we know it, teetered on the edge; just how scary and awful these times were. We must never forget what it felt like to live through Covid-19 in the year 2020.

This is the story of our history. This story attempts to capture the fear, the anger, the love, and the hope. The ways we looked for, and sometimes found, light in the darkness.

-

PROLOGUE

"And, He said, "Go out and stand on the mountain before
the Lord."
And behold, the Lord passed by, and a great and strong wind
tore into the mountains and broke the rock into pieces
before the Lord,
but the Lord, was not in the wind;
and after the wind an earthquake,
but the Lord was not in the earthquake.
and after earthquake a fire,
but the Lord was not in the fire,
and after the fire,
a still
small
voice."

1 Kings 19:11-13

~ 1 ~

SPANGLISH & CINDERELLA

2014, Orlando
His smooth, obsidian skin shines.
His strong shoulders flex.
The crisp, blue shirt of the TSA tugs at his biceps.
His quiet voice asks if she has taken off her shoes.
She responds with charades and eyes and voice
clearly of a different tongue.
"Zapatos?" He clarifies.
"Ah, si." She points.
"La Leche? Aqua?" He asks.
"No," she shakes her head.
As she and her hermana move through the check point.
Behind them, a man smiles and I think he looks like Jimmy Buffet.
In front, a woman with Florida-leather skin, bedazzled pockets,
hair in ball cap, fake boobs, chews gum
Exactly how a person
Should never
Chew gum.
She cackles a smokers laugh with her tanned, buff,
Tribal tattooed boyfriend.
No wedding rings.
They hurry for one last margarita.

The air smells of chlorine and sunshine
And Auntie Anne's pretzel shop.
I see Cubans and Asians, blacks, browns, coffee color,
Orange tans, blondes, ball caps,
Smiles for miles on the way in -
Exhausted families on the way out,
Wearing their Mickey Mouse ears
As the babies fall asleep in their strollers
Or cry out their exhaustion
As surely as their parents wish they could.
People hold doors, share phone chargers, move together
Going home to
Jamaica and Nebraska
Germany and Alaska.
All their beautiful combinations of Spanish, African,
Asian, European, Middle Eastern and everything in between
Mixes together and our language here,
In Florida,
In the sunshine state,
Is mostly Spanglish.
Dark eyelashes and eyebrows stretching for miles on blondes
With skin the color of caramel.
Tight curls in red hair
And coarse, black hair, straight as a bone.
No relaxer.
Deep set eyes on babies with thin lips,
And slight slants on blue eyes with full lips
Speaking of grits and Thanksgiving and house shoes at Gramma's.
And still, some look almost exactly like their
Great, great, great
Times 8
Ancestors must have.
Some DNA unchanged by migration
And slavery and colonialism and sun.

And here in the Sunshine State,
We come together to be with family
To see Mickey
To surf
To work
To play
And humanity shows us that there is no end
To the beauty of God's palette
There is no different
Or better
There just is.
A rainbow of life and love,
Mixtures and combinations that stretch the mind and heart
Where language is spoken fluidly
In several native tongues and Spanglish guides us all
In Florida.
In a country called America.
Where Tracy and Heidi and Kiki and Maria and Shalom
And Selah
And Tanisha
And Abuela
And Grandma
And Mimi
They
Make a rainbow
And they
Make
The Florida Sun
Shine.

-

~ 2 ~

PRIVILEGE

2016
Who are you?
I thought I knew.
I thought I knew you.
Somewhere between Head Bangers Ball and Yo! MTV Raps
I thought I met you.
Somewhere between Hurricane Katrina
And President Obama's inauguration night,
The TV glowed blue on my tear stained cheeks
As Beyoncé sang "At Last" my emotion, reflected in her eyes
Choking back tears and choosing the biggest smile instead.
Our innocent, idealistic eyes
That knew there were better days ahead
I thought I knew your heart
Like sunsets
Always changing and full of new color
Still reliable at the end of each day
Reminding me
That love always remains.
I thought I knew your soul.
Like family.
Diverse and loving,

Opinionated and not without its share of awkward politeness
In difficult times.
Some holidays we even skipped because it was just too much pain
To deal with on a holiday.
But still.
When tragedy struck
When hearts broke open
When sadness spilled
Like the slow molasses of open,
Awful,
Anguish,
Your soul was like family.
Like home.
Complete with a big hug from Momma to put you at ease,
And let you know that it would all be okay.
I thought I knew your hands like perfectly baked bread.
Thick and tender, just soft enough to peel apart
And nourish the tenderest tummy
Comfort the down-trodden and lead them straight to your shores
Yet, strong enough to hold the door,
Protect me from my hunger for love and closeness
The hard crust keeping the wolves at bay
To keep the faith that at the end of the day
Goodness would prevail.
I thought I knew your smell
Like my hometown city streets
The store front bakeries
With the scent of warm donuts filling the street
The Jiffy Lube smell of tires and oil
Jim's Rib Haven and the smell of a BBQ'd rack of ribs
The fall leaves crunching under feet
The rain.
Oh, the smell of the rain!
I thought I knew your story as well as I knew my own.

Your meager beginnings
Your bad decisions
The good ones that showed such grit,
Such determination,
Such beauty,
Such humanity.
Your ever bold march toward evolution,
Your own.
Toward kindness
Justice
Strength
Tolerance
Peace.
Now, I wake up to find
Your heart is not red with the beating blood of life and love
It is instead, an old, beat-up, pickup truck.
Rust pumping through your insides.
Black flecks appear to be everywhere,
Poisoning what was once a healthy collection of organs
Organisms
Your soul is suddenly turning inward to a dark place.
And when it turns outward again,
It snarls and bares its teeth
Moving toward the dark forces we all feel sometimes
Tugging at our insides
Sometimes.
Looking at the fear and believing it.
Looking at others and fearing them.
Looking at yourself and growing more arrogant by the minute.
You just love yourself so much
That others look small in comparison?!?!?!
The dark finds us all sometimes.
But you?!?!?
You were always so BRIGHT!

You were always so much better than that.
I feel like we're living in the upside-down.
You're the devout Christian turned atheist?
The atheist turned priest?
Your soul appears now, so self-serving.
So greedy.
So unaware of itself.
Then, there are your hands –
There is blood under your finger nails
A trunk full of sadistic tools
I catch a glimpse,
You slam the trunk
You tell me I'm imagining things
Those are for gardening
And that blood is just dirt
But, I know what I saw.
I know what I see.
That was the blood of your brother and those tools –
I know what they are for.
It cannot be gaslighted away.
Even your scent has changed.
You are all diesel engine and sour kraut.
Manure and sour milk.
Your story too, I can see it now – and it breaks things inside of me
That I did not know were there.
Your story has always been seen
Through the rose colored glasses of my love for you.
It has always been more bad decisions and brutality
With excuses
Than the beauty in my idealized image of you.
More selfish interest
Than truly concerned with doing the right thing.
It's just that the politics of the time were good for both.
But still.

I *believed.*
Really *believed* that you had gotten better
That you had changed.
I really believed it.
I changed with you.
We grew together.
Or so I thought.
And now I am faced with the horrifying truth.
The truth is – that I can finally see you.
My beloved America.
And I can finally see exactly who the fuck you are.

~ 3 ~

PINK

She said, "Maybe I need to wear more pink."
People always think I'm mean.
Or angry.
Her skin is dark
With diamond shine.
Her face wide.
Her eyes almond.
Set deep
Against cheek bones sharp enough to cut.
A smile wide and full.
Gap in her front teeth that tells a story
A history.
Ours.

She thinks and talks about deep things,
The metaphysical.
Energies.
The stars.
The celestial.
Horoscopes and Faith.
A connection to things bigger than this life,
Demonstrated in the way she walks.

Like a Queen.
She glides.
Graceful.
Her bones know her connection to this land.
Knows the land
Knows her.
In America, Virginia calls her.
She says she knows her people farmed that land.
By force.
In Africa, Ghana.
The place her DNA hails from.
Where she should be now.
Admiring oceans
Eating fish and cassava.
I wonder what her name would have been,
I wonder what beauty would have been hers,
Should have been hers.
Even though she is no doubt,
Beautiful here.
In Tennessee,
Raising babies,
And herself.
Alone.
Refusing the restrictions imposed by love
Doing it on her own instead.
At peace.
With her solitude.

But she's jumpy.
She's an Army veteran.
The trauma of her service
Of her lifetime
Of her lineage and history
Shows when a loud car revs its engine as it drives by.

I feel her fear.
I want to hug her.
I want to cry.
She is so gentle of spirit,
She almost whispers when she speaks,
But she is also tough,
Nothing can touch her and she knows it,
Not really.
We're just getting to know each other.
Really, know each other.
Moving from acquaintance to true friends,
Realizing our whole life has been a lie
Keeping like minded souls apart
By a country that has segregated everything
By race and class and religion
Neighborhoods
Jobs
Schools
Churches
Movies
Music
So that now,
We've lived in the same country for 40 years,
But we might as well have been across oceans,
Our lived experiences worlds apart.

But she has let me into her world,
And I've let her into mine
And as we did
We find our hearts circling the same moon
Searching for the same kinship
Both of us lonely
But finding alone
Easier than being in the world.

While I rage outwardly at truths she has always known
She retreats and finds an inner solace
A peace
She knows she cannot find in the world.

All I know, is a world that should bend to my demands,
I know a world where we organize and get groups together
And we can change the course of history.
I feel both a responsibility to make things change
And a belief that I can
Because the world has priveleged me
With some degree of fairness.
She knows a world that is anything but fair,
And she is teaching me about self love.
That rage will not protect you,
It will only steal your peace.
And protecting your peace
Is the only way to save your soul anyway.
And after all, isn't that the point?
Isn't that the purpose of this existence?
I am in awe.

She vibrates on a level above me
With a calm acceptance of things she cannot change
She has learned to love herself and protect herself
No matter what lies the world tells about her,
About "people like her."
She dances like no one is watching,
But I am.

She is teaching me things nobody has ever taught me,
An honoring of self,
A self assurance,

A belief in her divineness,
A beauty in femininity,
A wild, calm that cannot be contained
Or controlled
It cannot be stolen
Only given freely
And she knows to be selective
With such a gift.

I was not taught these lessons in self respect and love,
I was taught the opposite
The only reason to love yourself
Is if the world says you're lovable,
If the men say you're beautiful,
If the women say you're nice and pleasing and on the PTA.
There is a freedom in both of our existences
That the other does not have.
And she as Cancer and me as Capricorn
We are each others yin and yang,
And I am so sad that I wasted 25 years
Not knowing this friendship sooner.
Nobody I knew, knew how to build these bridges,
Everyone we knew, frightened of spaces where maybe,
They would not be welcomed.
But here we are,
Toni and Tina,
Pushing through walls
Our own
And other people's
To find
It was all a lie.

My peace will take years to find,
In the meantime,

In defense of her gentle toughness,
I will do everything in my power
To make the world
A place
Where she no longer
Feels like she needs to wear pink
To be seen,
For her gentle spirit to be understood,
Protected,
Safe.
I will use my privilege
And rage.

~ 4 ~

THE HILLS TURNED BLACK

December, 2018
The hills turned South Dakota
Black
The sky turned December
White
Tears streaked my cheeks
Like fireworks in the sky
On the Fourth of July
As my heart said its final,
Silent goodbye.
To Nebraska
And family
And forty years of friends
My brother,
The one who understands me best
Trusts me most
Helped us load all our things into a U-haul.
This U-haul
I'm sure he hates
As his best sister leaves him to fend for himself
Yet, he loads it anyway
With his best effort

Packed so tightly, nothing will break
As we leave
The land of the free
While the wind, the mountains
The water
The freedom
The healthcare
Calls to me
Changes me
Makes me
Who I always was anyway
A wanderer
A poet
A hockey fan
Looking for novelty
And faith
Trust and trees
Democracy
Freedom
From guns
And threat
And constant fear
Removing ourselves from the tapestry of our lives
feels like surgery
I weep as we drive.
For the jagged edges we leave behind
The blood loss,
An ugly scar remaining where once our family stood.
A scar in our neighborhood.
A scar in our kids' school.
A wound in our families.
That will never fully heal.
A missing piece of flesh from our lives.
Bitterness and sadness seep in filling the gap.

Where once, four people were.
Where we thought we were the same.
Americans.
An unwritten agreement that we believe in fairness and freedom
Kindness and equality
That racism is bad.
Democracy is good.
In 2016, we learned the truth about our place of origin
About our people.
And the truth,
It's ugly.
It's so much worse than we thought.
Our racism so much deeper and lasting.
Our belief in 'freedom' and 'democracy'
Only applies to those who look like us.
And we have dreams to pursue
And you can't pursue dreams there any more
The burning smoke of capitalism on fire and
Fake religion
Burning crosses
Is so thick
It chokes you
And forces you to focus on just
Surviving
There is no more time for dreams.
And the truth
Once you see it
You can't UNSEE it
So, we are cutting our family out of this fabric
Knowing the rips and tears will hurt.
Us
And the people we love.
Knowing it will be difficult.
Knowing my children and grand children will grow up

Canadian.
And that word evokes sadness for my children
Who will think things and say things and believe things
That I might not understand.
And that word.
"Canadian."
It also evokes
Gratitude
And gentleness
Kindness
Art
Music
Math
Science
Technology
Care and Love
And I know I am surgically removing
The stars and stripes from my heart
A cancerous tumor that must go.

-

~ 5 ~

OH CANADA

I have a favourite bird now
And a favourite tree
I am getting used to spelling all the words with a 'u'
And I can tell you temperature in Celsius, distance in kilometers.
My brain no longer short circuits when someone gives me
A postal code,
Or starts to mentally spell it out,
When someone says "Zed."
I have learned a winter hat is a toque
A sled is a toboggan,
Punjab is the northern part of India
Everyone in the whole world is here.
Including the Father of a medical student
studying in my home town
The best friend of my children's Omaha
eye doctor - also an eye doctor.
The world has grown
and shrunk in equal measure
In just 4 months.
The Queen reigns here
Still
And her face is on my money.

They follow rules here
And they read all the signs and do what they say.
And I'm not great at that.

But, in between taking deep breaths
I digest
Hateful Words
And spew them out to sea
Sailboats and float homes make them
Meaningless
Like your 13th mistress
Now,
I miss guessing at what this all means
I miss wondering if this is really happening
Now that I can breathe again.
I can see
clearly.
I know.
I am north of the border waiting for you to join me
Knowing, it won't be long
Knowing, I tried to secure your safety long before you could see it
Long before you could believe it
I don't have much.
But I have a stable for you.
A barn.
A tent.
A sleeping bag.
I have rice and beans for protein
Grapes and crackers and milk
I have Democracy here, too.
I have healthcare waiting.
Waiting for you to say that fear and racism and capitalism
For all its shine
On the surface

Covering the rust underneath
Waiting for you to know that freedom is worth it.
So, pick your favourite bird,
Pack your things
And listen to freedom ring
In your ears.
Pay attention to the direction
That bell tolls
From the north
And it's here
Waiting for you.

~ 6 ~

WHERE THE WILD THINGS ARE

There are mountains
And beaches here
And if you're from the very middle
Of middle America
That's everything.
So you think.
Because you went on vacation here twice
And you saw so many beach sunsets in those two weeks
Spanning 15 years
So you're sure you're going to love it here.
Looking back at your naïveté is already
Almost,
Funny.
And so is the way others say 'Neb ray skuh'
When they think they're speaking like Nebraskans.
Also, Nebraska is not Alaska
Or Arkansas
Omaha is not Oklahoma
Importantly, it was also part of the Union
Not the confederacy
I am not from 'the south'
And I didn't realize that was an important distinction to me

Until you asked why I didn't have a southern accent.
And now I realize the depth of the problems we're up against.
We're still living the original sin
Still fighting the same civil war.
Also, I realize
Starting over is harder than I thought would be
Of course.
When you've grown up in the same space
And lived there for a lifetime
And you've been raised to have your head on a swivel
To protect yourself from constant threat
Of guns
And guys
And people who don't look like you
And who pray differently than you
And who dress differently than you
And who have less money than you
As you realize that to be American
Is to be steeped in a fear of everyone.
Fear of our shadow at all times
A fear of our history,
One day, catching up to us
And holding us to account.
And you didn't even realize it until you crossed the border
And now you can tell,
You're always a little on edge
When you aren't familiar with your surroundings
When you're trying to raise two children
And tell them it's going to be okay
When you're watching your homeland become unfamiliar
But they've moved to a new country too
And nothing is the same here either
And *nothing* is familiar for a while.
You don't run into anyone you know.

Ever.
You don't recognize any streets or smells or places or people.
In fact, the opposite.
Everything smells different
And looks different
And sounds different
And people make eye contact at different moments
And apologize when you were least expecting it
And yell at you for talking on your cell phone while driving
Because I guess that's frowned upon here
But it took you 3 months to figure out why
They were yelling at you.
You thought maybe you were just driving too fast
Because the speed limit here is sooooo slow.
Nobody in a hurry.
It's Canada. The West Coast.
So, yes,
It's a lot.
Those first few months.
And then
The new wears off
And you run into your first familiar face at the grocery store.
And you're not frightened anymore
And
Now, that you're not scared
You start
to
See
The forest
Not just the trees.
And the way the kids talk about it – the forest
Like a
New friend
Not a place, but a person

Who is green
And has all the good and fun things
And they can wear their bedtime costumes
Playing hide and seek
Where their imagination lets loose
And the forest comes to life
And our dark and our light
Have room to play here
Safe
In
The
Forest.
Where all the Wild Things are.

-

~ 7 ~

MONEY MAKERS, MOVERS AND SHAKERS

First trip home since leaving
It's July 4th weekend and after our first Canada Day
The music and multiculturalism
Soul soothing
A day in the park, slight breeze,
lemonade,
live band,
weed.
The fireworks – non existent
To an American.
No children holding lit objects
No bombs bursting in air
No feeling of elation to have survived the night
All digits in tact.
In fact,
boring for a holiday celebrating your country's independence
To an American.
Where is the drama?
The noise?
The huge block parties?
The smell of burgers and gunpowder?

Is it even a summer holiday without those things?

The airplane reaches cruising altitude.
The peaks of mountains,
The vast expanse of the Pacific
Replaced below by patchwork, acres, agriculture.
The cool breeze of the ocean
Dissipates.
Replaced by the sweltering heat,
No breeze.
The thick smell of corn and farms
The man in the turban looks different here.
Vulnerable. Alone.
I have been gone just 6 months
After 40 years in the same place.
Spinning in circles
Twiddling my thumbs
Waiting to leave
And now that I have
I know I will never again fit in anywhere
Then again, maybe I never really did anyway.
But I am grateful for Spanglish at my layover
And for Swagger
And brush cuts
Enchiladas and big butts
I look like I belong here
My American diet
My American arrogance
My American edge
Here, I walk around like I own the place
I know this language
I speak this culture with my walk
I know now where this 'edge' came from
And how to use that edge to survive

Because here surviving is a constant struggle
There are no safety nets
We're all just flying on the trapeze, doing circus stunts
With nothing but creative, industriousness
And grit
And hustle.
Stateside
I am again protected by my passport
I live here, I was born here.
Mistakes here
Might get you killed
Gunned down
Wrong place, wrong time
Wrong picket line
Wrong cop
Wrong job
Wrong diagnosis
No healthcare.
But I can't be deported here
And it's weird to feel the relief
Of my birthplace
While simultaneously returning my head to its swivel.
I can live with abandon here.
I don't have to think or interpret culture here.
My instincts
Hard wired by a history written in my DNA
The Mayflower, The Oregon Trail
Yorktown & Bunker Hill
Washington & Lincoln
Sitting Bull & Pocahontas
Lewis & Clark
Cherokee & Sioux
The Trail of Tears & Jim Crow
Frederick Douglass & Cady Stanton

Martin & Mary J.
The Daughters of the American Revolution
And the Daughters of the Confederacy
Harriett Tubman & Ida B. Wells
Tulsa & Selma
Ogallala & Omaha
New York & Newtown
China Town & Little Italy
St Patrick's Day parades & Puerto Rican Day parades
The Quakers & the KKK
The Star Spangled Banner & the Super Bowl
Colin Kaepernick & Tom Brady
We're all here.
It's all here.

My Mom is here
And everyone I went to school with and played sports with
And worked with
And dated.
And so is every mistake
Every stupid thing I ever said
Every car accident
Every failed relationship
Every drunken fall
Every word said in anger
Every loss
Every death
Every ghost
I know now
'Home' will never mean what it once did.
Home will forever evade me now
Forever be an abstract
A feeling, an attitude
It is no longer a place

No longer an absolute
Something more like an idea
That I embody and just didn't know I did
Until I left it all behind
Until I could never be as kind as Canadians
Never as trusting or as thoughtful
Never as passive-aggressive.
I was not reared in a gentle place.
And harsh places don't produce soft people.
You can tell by my attitude
That I most definitely am
From America.
Home, is no longer a place, but a way of thinking
A way of walking
A way of being
More wrapped up in specific struggles, than specific streets
Home is now nowhere
And everywhere
Home will be wherever the struggle is
And my veins will always hold the struggle with me
In me,
Part of who I am.
The 'edge' of my upbringing – the losses and the wins
Infused in the land and people around me
As the plane touches down.
And with the struggle
The swagger
With the money makers
The movers and shakers
The decision makers, the name takers
There
I will always be
Home.

-

~ 8 ~

SNOW GLOBES

March 13, 2020
The whole world has become a time capsule.
We are frozen in time,
In our homes,
Stuck in a snow globe.
The world outside awaits us.
Alone.
While we spin inside listening to lullabies,
Catching snowflakes on our tongues
The streetlights outside long for traffic
The windmill spins with empty wind
The air longs for laughter
The parks long for children shrieking their delight
A basketball dribbling
A swing set creaking its joy.
Instead, we wait with Netflix and the Governor of New York
Explaining the expanse of the loss
We are living
We sit under the harsh light of our kitchens
Our living rooms
Poor posture
New work from home offices

Blue screens glow on our cheeks
For the lucky ones
The unlucky ones wondering where the jobs are
How to get one when you can no longer shake hands
How to feed their families when they can no longer work
The heroes -
"Always look for the helpers" they say.
Well, the helpers - they went to war.
A War without their permission
Without their knowledge that that's what they were signing
Up for
They will make the decisions now.
They will decide
Who lives and who dies.
Decisions they did not want to make.
The most educated, the most compassionate,
The best among us.
It is right that they will decide.
An unimaginable failure that they have to.
A failure of all of us, to protect them.
By voting for competence in our leaders.
A failure of Democracy for producing such stupidity
That now threatens to take us all out.
The unluckiest of all
Dead.
Alone.
Unable to breathe.
Unable to get a ventilator
Because
They Don't
Exist
Because capitalism won't save us.
In fact, capitalism has offered up our sacrifice.
Our grandmothers and grandfathers

Our undiagnosed diabetics
Those fighting cancer
and heart disease
Those heroes compassionate enough to try to save them
And dying for them instead.

Our calendars blink back tears of empty appointments
We can no longer keep
Our meetings are cancelled
Spring break camps that never were
Vacations never taken
Beaches never seen
Our blood work goes unchecked
Our massage will not happen
Our chiropractor is closed
Our nails will be ignored
Our hair grows long and grey
Our vanities are now all stripped away
And the truth is
We are all
So
Very
Ugly.
Outside and in.
We
Let this happen
Not **them**
Or **"those people"**
Or **that** country
WE
ME
YOU
US
We allowed the best and the brightest

The most compassionate among us
To be drafted into a war they did not ask for
From the decay of our own,
Personalized,
Hand held,
Snow globes
Filled with blue light
Where the sun never shines.

~ 9 ~

WE BURY OUR DEAD

April, 2020
We wake each day
To the sunshine
Brightening the day now
Bathing our rooms and our faces in light
Spring is coming
Birds are chirping
The sun awakens early now
Flowers are coming to life
Life is beckoning from beyond our window
Begging for us to come live it.
We still can't leave the house
So instead,
Every day,
We count
Our
Dead.
We call our Moms
We beg for mercy
From this cruelty,
This irony,
This sick,

Twisted fate.
The mercy comes in kindness from strangers
And neighbors
And sunshine
Each moment of mercy, a dagger.
A merciful, tortuous reminder that life goes on
That while we count our dead,
flowers are blooming in their name.
Birds are chirping their existence -
A reminder that we are still alive
A reminder that the entire world is counting on you
To live
Not just to live,
But we need you
To live well.
To plant a garden,
To do your job and do it well.
To raise your children and raise them well.
Teach them all the things they will need to know
Like how to spell 'definitely beautiful,'
And how to wash their hands properly,
20 seconds at least,
Soap and water,
Don't forget your thumbs,
Do it twice if you must.
Teach them how to be generous with their time,
Selective with their minds,
Focused with their attention,
Especially with Grandma and Grandpa.
Each phone call
Aware that it could all end in a day,
A week,
A month.
Praying for the calendar to flip to 2021 as quickly as it can

With as little loss as possible
And even that will be an
Insurmountable loss
Greater than our collective hearts can bear.
We have so much time now

And so

.....little

...........else

The clock moves mercilessly on the wall

Tick tock
                Tick tock
Tick tock

A reminder that we have no choice but to go on living
To put one foot in front of the other
To pick up one body bag after another
Because someone must
Get out of bed,
Take a shower and go
Bury the dead
Bring bread to the living
Someone must
Go
On.
So, we find joy in the song the neighbor plays
In the artwork children hang in windows
In the sound of the breeze
The sight of the sun
We find joy and love where we can

And we bask in it,
We savor it and
We watch it go too soon.
Each day.
As we bury our dead.

-

~ 10 ~

GROWING UP COMPLICATED

One day, in the spring of 2020,
She woke up
With a greasy face, a swollen nose, darker eyebrows.
That day, she woke up,
Complicated.
She cried for no reason three times that day.
And my normally, well-adjusted, easy-going, oldest
Has a well of emotion and thoughts that need expression,
That have no home,
That she needs to let out.
As though her body knows
As surely as the adults around her know
That a global pandemic during her grade 3 year
Will soon rage uncontrolled in her homeland
That a global pandemic during her grade 3 year
Means, she is going to have to grow up quickly,
Before her time,
Differently,
Than anyone alive today could prepare her for.
She, as the oldest child,
And a girl,
Is going to have to pay attention to the world around her

In ways that seemed unimaginable
The day she was born in 2010.
When we enjoyed sports and endless parties and weddings
And watched ESPN and American Idol
And had no idea what the office of government ethics was
Or what our congressional district was
Or who our Attorney General was.
Now, this past stupidity feels like a warning -
A precursor of what was to come.
And also, a blessing.
A day, when you could trust things
To run without your never ending attention -
Without your picket signs,
Your bodies in the street.
When we lived in a giant home, with a sprawling back yard
And spent gobs of money on dinners and parties and birthdays.
When, for her first birthday,
We celebrated with an Elmo cake
And a large, extended network of friends and family members –
60 in all.
Because she was turning 1.
The years before it all fell apart.
The years before reality strained every friendship group,
Every family.
The years before we understood,
That we were at the beginning of the end,
Or the end of the ending of a beautiful, prepackaged chapter
That now feels more like a highly successful
Marketing campaign
Than a time of true friendship and comradery.
The performative acts of friends and family
That fooled us
Into thinking
We wanted the same things

That we could share space and a country without conflict
Now, we know that in the 'sharing'
There is death.
A tug of war
Kill or be killed
An eye for an eye
And now the whole world is going blind.
In 2020, the ignorance and arrogance – the lack of any empathy
Or experts in the room
Has now arrived as a real threat to our very lives
Just as we told them it would.
And we were told we were being hysterical,
We know now our children will pay the price
Lose their families
Their grandparents
Their childhood.
The crises that was predictable,
Because crises are always predicted
When corruption is in charge,
It has happened.
It has arrived.
And now it is her problem.
Because she's almost 10 and it's clear that the world is
Being remade
Under her feet
While she ties on the ballet slippers of blooming
And gets ready to dance
The dance of womanhood
While she borders on becoming
Her mind and body and soul are intrinsically aware
That it's time
For her to grow up.
Complicated.

~ 11 ~

MOLASSES DOWN A
MOUNTAIN SIDE

I could have never guessed that
When the world was ending
It would end
In
Slow
Motion.
Like Molasses dripping down a mountain side
I never imagined,
During the end times
We'd still have
So much
Time.
To enjoy
A Sunset
A Kiss
A Beer
A Hug
A Song
An Eagle
Soars Above my Head
My heart attaches to its wings

My son plays the piano
My husband's silhouette smiles.
I shadow box the Devil and
Tell him
Not.
Yet.

The air smells fresh,
My hair is done for the first time in months,
I'm getting a tan on the back patio,
And talking to my Mom
And the neighbours.
From a distance
6 feet apart
Waving and laughing and missing breaking bread together
But this is not as bad as it could be
As I imagined it would be
I am
Writing Poetry
Rockin' Tom Petty
And a Tank Top
Wondering about my blood work
And the kids' schoolwork
And if I'll have work
And
And
And
And
And
Enjoying the last
Of
This
Life
As hundreds of thousands across oceans

Struggle to breathe
I pay homage
With all the love I can believe in
In my home
On my deck
With my family
We plan vacations for 'some day'
And careers for 'when this is over'
And when we'll buy a home 'after the pandemic'
And when we'll finish university in person
And I can't believe I've started saying in that way.
Because
Someone. Must. Live.
Because
Someone. Must. Love.
Because
If the world is ending
It ends in slow motion
And
There
Is
Still
So
Much
Time
To
Live.

~ 12 ~

WE. CAN'T. BREATHE.

Memorial Day Weekend - 2020
It has been just over 60 days
Of silence and stillness
Stuck in our homes
With nothing to do, nothing to watch
But a daily,
Growing
Body count.
With the summer coming,
With our stir crazy stirring,
Our Cabin, fevering
On Memorial Day,
Minneapolis,
For 8 minutes
46 seconds
The life drained out of a man
On video
Under the knee of a smug man in blue
Again.

The fucking lid blew off.
It is a summer of righteous rage.

A summer where there will be no quiet.
There will be no Peace.
Because there is no Justice.
The boots have arrived to our city streets
The boots we knew were coming.
Tear gas and batons gnash their teeth on bare flesh
Flash bangs warn of worse fates.
Fascism live on Twitter and Facebook.
Beating bodies holding signs and freedom
Our innocent, American stares
Blink away tears
And tear gas
Dousing our eyes in milk
Armed with
Nothing
But
Milk
Because
We don't know a country where we would need to be armed
To protest
But only because we didn't listen to the sounds of our ancestors
Or we thought something had changed.
We learned, in 2020, nothing has changed.
We would be reminded again,
The lessons of the 60's
The water hoses and the dogs
The white women and Ruby Bridges,
Bloody Sunday
And Letter from a Birmingham Jail.
The bullshit they told us in our history books
About the First Amendment
And the right to peaceably assemble
To address our grievances
Would come face to face

With facts.
That the amendment was written for white, male, land owners
And anyone else, will be beaten if you try
To assemble
To demand redress to grievances
But we brought our signs and our demands anyway.
We stood on the shoulders of our ancestors
We carried our children on our back
We got smarter and tougher every week
We started bringing equipment to protect ourselves.
Skateboards
And helmets
And homemade shields from trashcan lids
We learned how to be street medics,
Protect our eyes from intentional head shots
With rubber bullets
We learned how to tourniquet wounds from night sticks
We funded attorneys and bail money
Wrote bail phone numbers on limbs with sharpies
We were kettled in alleyways and residential areas
And interstate bridges
Like enemy combatants.
Women and children in strollers,
Clergy and Rabbi
Teenagers and Elders
Attacked for existing,
For assembling,
For protesting,
For demanding Justice
For believing we had the right to not be murdered
In the streets.
We kept coming back for months
We brought cans of food – to eat and to throw
We

Don't
Want
To hurt
You
We wish the feeling was mutual.
Our hearts scream for justice
After Rodney King
And Eric Garner
Trayvon Martin
Tamir Rice
And Mike Brown
Alton Sterling
And Rayshawn Brooks
And Philando Castille
And Sandra Bland
And Breonna Taylor
And George Floyd
The list of names – the video imagery –
A constant trigger warning
A pressure valve of injustice
A fireball of flames and fury
Ready to explode.

After incompetence and ambivalence
Killed 100 thousand of us
Destroyed the livelihoods of millions,
We were all sent home
To stay inside
And think about what we've done.
No more sports
No more dinner parties
Or birthday parties
Nobody left but you and your family
Or your loneliness

Or whatever life you have created so far
To just look you in the face
And ask you if you've created one that you love
If you've created one that you can sustain
And in our 60 days of stillness
In our 60 days of silence
We.
Finally.
Listened.
To the screaming inside our hearts.

The beast in us has awakened to find
That we are a people under siege
By corruption
And indifference
By authoritarian policing and unprovoked violence
You are stealing the future from us all
And, now it is your turn to hear us.
Our mouths are no longer taped shut
Our hands no longer bound
We finally smelled the stench of your lies
The rot inside your soul
And we are performing surgery
A malignant tumor that must go.

The blood work showed this could happen
We all knew this cancer could grow again
And then we just watched it grow.
We ignored the lump in our throats,
We ignored the knot in our guts,
We cannot ignore it any longer.

Your knee on our necks
Your virus spreading uncontrolled

Your unidentified soldiers on our streets.
We. Can't. Breathe.

This is not freedom
This is capitalism you cherish.
This is not religion,
This is a golden calf.
You are worshipping dollars over justice,
Order
Over peace.
The veil has fallen and fallen fast
But perhaps not fast enough
Because we are waking up to understand
That power never cedes power
Power must be taken
It must be organized
It must be earned
While we choke through your tear gas,
We take your beatings in the street.
While we bury our dead,
We fall to our knees in prayer for His mercy.
We stand with fists in the air for Justice,
We walk the streets in our masks,
Jobless and hungry
Angry and righteous
And filled with a rage for Justice.
Filled with a demand for our lives
Filled with fists full of petitions
To get your knee off our necks
Get your boots out of our streets
Because in our blood
In our roots
In OUR boots
Is the lineage of the most courageous among us

The strongest among us
The bravest among us
We are the ones you could never kill
We are the seeds planted by our ancestors
Now in full bloom
And ready to take our rightful place in history
Ready to demand atonement in the streets
Atonement at the ballot box
We wait on bated breath
For November 3rd
To answer the biggest question
We've ever been asked.
Will we succumb to tyranny?
Will we let them steal Democracy?
Freedom?
Self Determination?
Will we let them intimidate
And frighten
And jail us
And kill us
Until we stop fighting?
Or will we fight back?
Will we demand freedom
For ALL of us
Yearning to Breathe Free?
Will we stand firm with our neighbors
Our friends
Our family
Our brothers
Our sisters?
Will we demand and remain steady
That if there is
No Justice,
there can be no peace?

Because
We
Can't
Breathe.

~ 13 ~

LANTERNS

There are people in this world
That light the way
Bright and unassuming
Humble and kind
Beautiful and perfect.
You know them when you meet them -
They are the epitome of 'awkward' sometimes,
They are the funniest people you'll ever meet.
But their jokes are told quietly,
To a small audience,
Under their breath.
There is no flash.
There is nothing about them that is fake.
There is nothing contrived.
They really do care about you,
About others,
About people.
They lose their shit some days just like the rest of us,
But they don't lose sight of others.
Always thinking about them,
Reaching out to them,
Hoping to please them,

Lift them up,
Light them up with joy,
With happiness,
With hope,
With a future,
With belief,
They point the way
Through the darkness.
They point the way
With an internal light.
That radiates.
Shines.

They look to the Heavens
They rely on their humanity
They don't respond to gravity
Nothing can hold them down
Nothing can breathe them in
But everyone can see them
Everyone delights in their joy
Delights in their journey.
Everyone watches and waits for them
To glance upon them
To be touched by their grace
Their wisdom
Their willingness to care for others
And their ability to do so.
I have known them
I have taken them for granted as most do
I have wondered at them
I have appreciated them
I have marveled at their kindness
Their thoughtfulness.
I have said prayers for them

I have rejoiced for them
I have seen their beauty so reflected in the world
I have hoped that they live for thousands of years
Because they deserve to
They should
They do.
They, are like stars
They, are the ones
Who are made in His image I am sure
More so than the rest of us probably
If I'm honest.
The helpers
The thoughtful ones
The kind ones
The sacrificial ones
The 'give you the shirt off their back ones,'
The 'call you just to see how you are' ones,
The 'I don't need recognition and actually, please don't' ones.
The lanterns in this life.
Lighting the way
Rubbing your back
Lifting you up
Lighting the sky
Showing you beauty
Making you believe
And see
And wonder
And hope
And laugh
Showing you love
And you know who you are.
But don't worry, I won't tell.
My beautiful,
Hopeful,

Humble,
Kind,
Honest,
No Drama,
Love Mantra,
Light the way,
Leaders,
But softly,
Lanterns.

Dedicated to those health care workers and essential workers who lost their lives during the Covid pandemic.

~ 14 ~

HELL HATH NO FURY

September, 2020
I broke in front of them.
I unleashed a fury inside my soul
While they looked on.
And I think the thing that makes me most angry
Is that you expect me not to be
Angry.
How could I not be angry?
What kind of human doesn't get angry
When people are murdered in the streets?
What kind of person doesn't get angry
When babies are torn from their mothers' arms
Weeping and begging for mercy?

And, so in the summer of rage
I embraced my own.
And I will not be nice
And I will not pretend any longer
That I am okay with this arrangement.
I will lace up combat boots
Shave the side of my head
Put on black eye liner

And red lipstick
And mouth
FUCK YOU FOREVER
Having said that,
I feel a little better now.

Sure, there are spots that have moved me,
Soothed me.
Given me space to grieve,
Space to rage,
The rights to my anger
Like a copyright from the library of congress
I own this.
And I don't apologize.
I descend into a dark place with serpent tongues
The walls ablaze
And some nights I like it there.
I come up for air sometimes and when I do
I take big, deep, gulps of life-giving oxygen,
Of mountains
Of trees
Of sun and sky
Where my mind turns words over and over again
"In my defense, I have none."
"March, march, to my own drum."
"I am not throwing away my shot."
I scream in the face of all these "nice white women"
Because
I've been having dark dreams for a long time.
Ever since
The first knuckled, ringed,
Back hand
Hit my face,
And bloodied me at 3

For lying about brushing my teeth
And then told me to lie about it and say I ran into a tree,
This rage has been on a slow simmer
For a lifetime.
Of living in a patriarchy that values me less
That values my abuse and labels it 'civil society'
And 'keeping our neighborhoods safe.'
Safe for who?
It has NEVER been safe for me!
And on some level I had even grown to accept the abuse.
After all, what choice did I ever have?
But the idea that you get to abuse us all like this
And then tell us we can't even be angry -
That is the point where I broke.
When I was denied even the right to be furious about the abuse
This was the final straw.

I descended into a furious pit lined with women
So angry and ugly
We lose all value,
Because we all know,
There is no value in an angry, ugly woman
To a society that has determined our worth
In being beautiful
And pleasant
And pliant.
But to be fair
There is no value in an angry, ugly, aggressive man either.

There is only war.

Which is now what you have.
And I guess that's what you wanted.
We're going to need Taylor Swift to release another album.

But even she is furious these days.
So instead, I put on songs of the revolution
I lace up my boots
And I March.
Because I've already been abused
So now, I might be abused and angry
But mostly, I am
Now,
Just completely
Unafraid.

~ 15 ~

DANCING IN THE RAIN

The fires have started
In the south
The Earth burning just as scientists have always said it would.
The smoke has filled the sky
And stolen the September sun
Stolen the air
Stolen the beach
Stolen the mountains
Stolen days,
Weeks,
Months,
Lungs,
Lives.
The sky reflects how dire the situation feels
How dire it is.
The world is burning
Literal and Metaphorical
Getting hotter every year
It's hard to perceive in real time
But in months like this
When acres are caught in an inferno
And ash fills the sky

Smoke sticks to your clothes
And fills your nostrils.
There it is
Plain as day
In front of our face.
The daylight -
The sun,
Blotted out.
Stolen.
For weeks.
By smoke and flame
Our masks now, dual purposed
A foggy mess threatening the lungs of our children
Forcing us to stay inside.
Again.
Urging us to act
And all we can do is wait
And pray
For rain.
And sometimes
Prayers delayed can feel unheard -
Can seem ignored
But today,
On this day,
The blue sky poked through,
The sun shone
And it finally,
Mercifully,
RAINED!!!!!!
It washed away the smoke
And the bleak
And we looked up
Let it wash our face
And combine with our tears

To make some new chemistry
Of smoke and rain
And love and grief
And we danced
While the sky
And our eyes
Wept.

THE DAY HIS FEVER SPIKED

The day his fever spiked.
His face went white
First.
Then mine.
With fear.
He had a cough that morning
Fresh out of bed
I told myself he just needed water from the sleepy night
Some water and he was fine.
Just a normal morning of Fortnite and YouTube.
A typical quarantine kids morning.
At 1pm, he came to my side while I worked.
Tapped my arm.
Urgent in his expression.
Eyes wide and big and grey
Full of eyelashes
Fear coloring his irises darker
Than their usual shade of green.
"Mom, what if when I go to sleep,
I can't breathe? Will you know?"
An awareness that an 8 year old baby shouldn't have.
But of course they do.

It's been months now of a new life.
And now, the thing that changed the world with quarantines
And no school, no birthday parties,
A constant, growing death toll,
Parents baking sourdough bread,
Working from home,
Becoming home school teachers
Cheering for health care workers every evening at 7pm.
Of course he knows.
From his wide-eyed expression I know
That he knows
He is going to know 'the thing.'
We have tried so hard to avoid.
He knows and I know he has Covid.
Because me and this boy
Have always known each other inside out
Like from another life or dimension together
With him, I just 'know.'
"Mom, I don't feel good," he said.
I brush his stubborn hair to the side of his head
It never wants to part to, but at some point when he was 2,
We had to pick a side and we went with it.
His hair never did.
"Don't worry buddy, just get some rest and drink some water.
Probably just a little cold."
Fever 100.7.
No color.
Cough starting more frequently.
Sinuses stuffed up.
I immediately took a lunch break
From my at home laptop and race to the pharmacy
To get some medicine.
A panic in my chest knowing the hospitals are full
Knowing I don't have health insurance

Knowing the wealthy and privileged survive
And we are mostly, middle class at best
Our odds
50/50.
The panic rising in my throat tastes like metal
Like bile,
Like blood.
I call the doctor.
Earliest appointment is in 3 days.
I start asking myself the lengths I will go to save my child.
Who will I call, how much will I spend?
Would I threaten someone else if I had to?
Would I kill to save him?
Yes.
Just like when I was pregnant with this boy
I didn't need a test to confirm, I knew he was a boy
And I know he has Covid.
I hadn't seen a mask for days on anyone but us
I don't know why others didn't love him -
This beautiful, sweet boy -
Don't want to protect him with simple gestures, but they didn't.
They were consumed with themselves I suppose.
They were down in rabbit holes alone and angry
Believing insanities and absurdities.
The stranger we had tried not to know,
Now we were going to have to meet.
We were going to have to wonder about our predispositions.
Our genetic material.
Would we hold up?
What will its impact be to his body, my family,
His lungs, his heart, his liver, his kidneys, our lives,
My heart.
There are no words for this kind of unknown.
There are no words

For seeing your baby in the jaws of an alligator
And in slow motion
You
Must
Wait
To
See
If
It
Bites
Down
Or
Lets
Him
Go

There is only fear.
And a Mother's Love
And a Hail Mary
That it will be enough.

~ 17 ~

CURTAINS AND CHORUSES

The sounds of grief and loss
Joy and dance
Human resilience in every song.
Every verse.
Every note.
Art sustained us when it all collapsed.

Yo Yo Ma vibrated bow across cello strings,
Music flooded balconies in impromptu concerts,
Broadway stars and opera singers performed,
Wherever they could
For their neighbors.
For humanity.
Every old and new song filled the heart
With so much sadness of all the things we were losing
Even as we lost it.
Underneath,
A belief,
A sneaking suspicion,
That maybe we were gaining something too.
Although we did not yet know what it was.
Luke Combs and "6 feet apart"

Alec Benjamin, same title.
Lump in throat,
Eyes welling up,
Even Taylor Swift spoke in deeper, hushed tones.
Slower.
The sound of the quietest melodies
Still so loud in this new silence.
Folklore, Evermore
A string of gold
Tying us all together in our grief
Our loneliness
Our homespun dresses.
With each new song
The tears
The sadness
The beauty of the life of innocence we had before 2020
The beauty of things that used to seem
Normal, boring, annoying, obligations
Now look like utter privileges we took for granted.
Meals with our friends
Church with our families
Sporting events
Kids activities
School
Coworkers
First kisses
Holding hands
Hugging strangers
Shaking hands.
The loss of human touch and connection changed us slowly,
Every day.

Every now and then, we would forget
And we would hug or shake a hand

And then
You knew you shared a secret with someone.
An affair of social graces.
You cheated.
You shared a risk.
A recognition that you might die for them
For the need to be human again.
To touch,
To express affection and love and appreciation for them.
Your smile and familiarity with one another
Forever,
Changed.

Throughout the spring and summer of 2020
Anyone who had the basic of musical interest or talent,
Shared it from their homes
With the windows flung open
Curtains and choruses billowing out
To fill empty air,
Starving hearts.
It was a blessing
A gift.
The art, the music -
A life raft when you were drowning.
CPR to your spirit,
A defibrillator just when you thought you'd flatlined
And reminded us
What humanity feels like.
The grief was so heavy
Because life and love and art
Are just so fucking beautiful
It hurts.

Unknown if you'd be there to appreciate it all next year,

Next month,
Next week,
Tomorrow.
And by the time we got to winter 2020
Mariah Carey was new again.
A new meaning to an old song.
"All I Want For Christmas is You"
And this year,
It was not a cliché
It was not a Christmas song
It was not about your lover.
In the year 2020, this song was now the truth.
And we all just wanted the "you" that was everyone.
Everyone we loved.
Every family member.
Every friend.
"You" was now a metaphor for every year prior.
A past life of innocence and joy.
The time before it all fell down.
"You" was everything we took for granted.
Couldn't have conceived of how much we had to lose back then.
And all we wanted for Christmas in 2020,
Was "You."

~ 18 ~

OLD PICTURES

Old pictures
Old flames
Time burns the back of my throat.
The second hand,
Breaks my heart
The hour hand carves out my pride.
Reminds me of a place and time
Where this mess
Was so clean.
When we were all still friends,
When families were still together
Before him.
Before this.
Before we forgot.
Or before it was revealed.
Who we were.
Who we are.
I sit
Beside myself
Searching for lost joys
Remembering music and concerts and goodness and my brothers
And my Mother

And my Sister
Before we were all so sad.
Before we knew the truth of our differences.
We try and talk about the weather and how we miss sports
And family
And hugs
We try and talk without mentioning
How we used to live
How it used to be
Before him – Voldemort,
He who shall not be named.
And we all know I told you so,
As I railed against this part of us,
Yes us - all of us.
This ugly, ugly part of us
That now, threatens to take us all down.
This part of us, that can be activated
With just the right precision
The perfect combination of anger and fear and racism
That will have my brother accusing me of treason
While I weep for babies to not be held in cages
Torn from their Mothers' arms, wailing,
Just as I am tucking mine into warm beds.
When we lived with abandon and hugged with no regard
Back when we just loved.
And lived.
And there weren't 180K dead
And I hadn't revised that number 10 times in 6 months.
Back when there weren't protests every night
And we all knew that there weren't 'good people on both sides'
And your country heart
And your red neck
Just wanted to make your home town proud
And keep your family safe

And help your neighbor
And now
Here
We
Are
Where we bow our heads
And clasp our hands
And close our eyes
And talk to God.
I beg for Him to put love back into our hearts
Put commitment to each other,
To the little guy, the under dog,
The tired and the poor
The huddled masses,
Into our country again.
I pray for powers beyond mine
To soften our hearts
For one another.
To find the goodness in us all
And nurture it,
Water it,
Help it once again grow,
And bloom.

There is no joy in this.
There is no joy in the, "I told you so,"
While grandparents and children,
Struggle for breath, alone in hospitals
While our minds long for rest,
For peace
For calm
For quiet
For trust
For faith in a system

That has been destroyed
From the inside out.

There is no happiness in school closures
Or counting our dead.
There is no gloating
In watching your countrymen kill each other.
With incompetence
Corruption
Conspiracy theories
Disinformation
Guns.

There is no joy in watching a beautiful country succumb
To greed
And hate
And fascism
And death
And unabashed
White Nationalism.
Even if you saw it coming.
Especially if you saw it coming.

There is also no denying that it's happening
Especially, when you get outside of the borders
And you're looking outside in.
When you're watching from a country filled with immigrants,
And you are one.
A country filled with people
Who become friends
And colleagues
And neighbors
Who have fled worse fates
In more recent generations

Who tell you how this reminds of them what happened
In Iran in the 70's
When the religious right took over their government,
Or Brazil in recent years with corruption,
Or a caste system in India.
The looks of sympathy
And empathy
And deep, deep
Concern and worry
Canadians share
At the grocery store
At children's soccer games
In our neighborhood
When we meet
And they hear my accent
And confirm I am from America
Is life altering.
Is genuine.
Is so very sad.
"What is happening to your country?" they would ask.
"How are you?"
"Is your family okay?"
"How is this happening?"
I almost always answered,
"Facebook."

Canadian culture,
I have learned,
Is steeped in a love of nature
The Maple Leaf
Means something.
It means,
Spend time in the trees,
See the mountains

Go breathe in the beach.
Every day.
Get a daily dose of Vitamin D
Go touch grass.
We could learn a lot from our neighbours
To the North.

They were are all longing
For vacations again to Florida and California
New York, Hawaii and Vegas
The places and people they loved
So fun and vibrant
Full of everyone and everything
They would look at their old pictures
Of an America
That is almost becoming unrecognizable.
But more than a vacation,
They were longing for your safety,
For your freedom,
For you to realize what is happening to you,
Before it's too late.

Before all we have left
Is old pictures.
Of the country you used to be.

~ 19 ~

12 HOURS

The church bells rang in Paris.
There were fireworks in London.
The entire world let out a collective gasp.
A sigh of relief that instantly
Confirmed the truth.
Instantly,
Ended the gaslighting.
Instantly,
We became aware
Just how long we'd been holding our breath,
Clenching our teeth,
Tension in our entire global body,
Released.

Headlines said things like,
'Welcome Back America,' and,
'An enormous relief for Europe.'
In a German publication,
An image of President Biden,
Puts the Statue of Liberty's head
Back on her body.

Seeing the world rejoice,
Seeing the countries who know the devastation of demagogues,
The wreckage or war,
The insidiousness of hate,
Seeing that the whole world knew
And understood,
How effective propaganda is
At infecting human hearts,
With hate
Fills me with an empathy
For what they once lived through.
Makes me newly aware
Of a truth we now share.
We know now
How effective lies, with slick marketing,
Are at radicalizing an entire people.
Even the most freedom loving, democratic, immigrant people.

Because the world has seen this before
We wrote it down.
We begged you to 'Never forget'
But the lessons just got lost
And twisted
And people put 'Never Forget'
In their minds to mean
'Germans, don't forget.'
Because we think we're different here.
Special.
Super human.
Americans.

Not seeing the parallels
REFUSING to see the parallels.
But the lesson,

The 'never forget'
The stages,
The steps,
Towards fascism
Where *everyone* loses,
Has been underway for at least 4 years now,
And those places who have lived through its destruction before
They know.
They know what it sounds like.
They know what it feels like.
They know how the air around you changes.
They know how the people around you change.
They know,
Fascism is a can of worms sprung open,
You can't get back into the can.
It is Pandora's box.
It will become a monster in the hearts of men
That you cannot contain.
'And then it will come for you.'
This was the 'Never Forget.'
That we forgot.
More likely,
That we never truly learned.
Now we understand,
Intimately aware,
It can happen to anyone.
It can happen anywhere.

So, on this night, four days after the election
November 7th
A winner was declared
And, for the first time in 4 years
We felt maybe, enough of us,
Did learn something from history.

We learned not to wait.
We learned this was no time for neutrality.
We learned no one was coming to save us.
We learned about the fierce urgency
Of now.

We learned, not to sit still,
We learned to organize and act!
We voted for our lives,
AND IT WORKED!
And after 4 years and 4 days of holding our breath
Clenching our jaws,
Knocking on doors,
Calling our Senators,
Protesting in the streets,
Fighting back with the truth,
For 12 hours on November 7th
We exhaled.
We rejoiced that, maybe, we slayed the dragon
Before it breathed the fire of hate all over everything
And burned it all down.
Before the monster in us all
Took us all to the depths of hell
And refused to let go.

And that night, for one night,
It felt like,
Our innocence returned.
Our desire for love
And kindness
And peace
And to just be
And to live free
And for political heat,

To leave our living rooms
To stop threatening our very existence
Our friendships and families
And instead, to exist in the halls of Congress
Where it belongs.
For one night,
Our love and joy and feelings of safe harbor returned.
Safe with each other,
Safe with our lovers,
Safe in our homes,
Safe in our skin.

On this night
For 12 hours
There was joy in the tweets
And dancing in the streets.
We had harnessed our voices
And our power and we
Voted
His
Ass
Out.

That beautiful Saturday night
11/7
All the things we learned in Kindergarten were true again
Honesty matters
Integrity matters
Don't lie
Don't cheat
Treat people how you would like to be treated
Share.
Good will always prevail over evil
Here, right matters.

Kindness matters.
Goodness matters.
And
Joy
And
Art
And
Music
And
Love
Returned.
For 12 hours.
And the world rejoiced.
And breathed
A sigh of relief

The weight of which,
Contained all of human history.

~ 20 ~

REMEMBER. LIGHT.

It's late November now.
The cold
The snow
The winter
Which normally is beautiful
And cold
And slow.

But this year
It's something different.
Dark.

We are still inside
Still alone
Tears come in unexpected intervals
As the grief and loneliness tugs
At frayed threads of
Errant nerves.

The time drags on.
So many lives have been lost.
The snow - a reminder of death.

The slow - a reminder of loneliness
And endless hours and lost days
That transcend words.
We begin to prepare our tables for holiday feasts.
So many tables are missing someone,
Multiple someones.
Fractured lives, families
Survivor's guilt – grateful if your family has made it
Guilty if you're grateful.
We have still not properly laid to rest our dead.
It's a year where we ask
How much sadness can fill one year?
One month?
One week?
How many awful things should we endure?
Thanksgiving, into Christmas
Even the lovely things have become tinged with awful.
Weddings without the guests.
Birthday Parties in the car.
No hugs. Just horns.
We tried to make the best of it.
But, every human moment, a risk.
Bat mitzvah on zoom
Wedding remotely.
Her Dad couldn't walk her down the aisle.
Immunocompromised, asthma.
Another wedding cancelled. Next year they said.
No graduations will be held,
No prom,
No high school sports,
No gatherings over 10,
How many funerals were done online?
Not even COVID funerals.
Just regular funerals,

For your Mom, your brother, your aunt, your sister
Who lost a battle with cancer, heart disease,
Car accident, depression.
You couldn't get home,
You couldn't be there.
You couldn't travel and even if you could travel
It didn't make sense to get there.
Quarantine for 14 days
And then miss the funeral anyway.
Then come back,
Quarantine again for 14 days.
The strain and heaviness of the grief
The loss unrecognized, uneulogized
Almost 12 months now
Is all so terrible, so never ending
We all wonder if things will ever be 'normal' again
Will we ever have a holiday season full of innocence and joy?
This one,
Is the saddest,
Loneliest ever felt.

The usual happiness and excitement of the holidays
Replaced with a lonely, dread.
It will be a holiday.
But it will be just another day,
Another Tuesday or is it Sunday?
Spent with only those in your home
No travel, no big family gatherings
And while the hustle and bustle of the season will be slowed
It will not feel like a holiday at all
It feels more like a funeral.
And the day after will be just another day
Just like the day before.

So isolating
So broken
So up-ended
So
Fucking
Sad
Everything that had made everyday life important
And beautiful
And broken up the monotony of just,
Regular life
Is now,
Not allowed.
And those brief moments
Where you had too much to drink
And you snuck in some abandon
And you hugged
Or shared the chips and dip
You knew you were risking
Your entire family
And the guilt nagged even at your drunken mind
The joy
Always dimmed with a knowing.
The sadness
Always lurking
Hanging over your shoulder
Like a shadow you couldn't shake
Like a cello always playing in B flat
The endlessness of it,
For an entire year,
Longer.
Corpses littered our lives,
Death always at the door step,
The joy dimmed on the joyous days,
Always reminding us of all we've lost,

All we were losing,
Every
Single
Day.

Firsts and lasts
We'd never get back.
A permanence to this history that will always be.
Births celebrated without grandmas
Grandmas saying goodbye
Alone
On zoom.
Cancer patients going to appointments alone,
Surgeries completed with no family at their side,
Holidays and birthdays celebrated alone,
Or far away,
Or without hugs,
Or with accompanying funerals.
Proms missed,
Homecomings past,
Never to be redone.
No grad,
No senior trips,
No overnights at camp,
So much nervous energy.
No parties,
No gyms,
No events,
Just you.
Bouncing around
Wondering what to do with yourself
Just you
And your four walls
And those people and things within your four walls.

No exceptions.
And if you made exceptions
You paid for it
You died for it
You killed for it
You spent weeks hospitalized for it
And then realized it wasn't worth it.
Always too late.
Always with a softened tone.
A wistful memory of your innocence -
When you didn't know life could be this cruel -
When you didn't know dark could be THIS dark.

You expected at the beginning that at some point
You might only be left with a lamp.

And eventually, you accepted there might just be a candle.

But by the end,
You were hanging on to the burning embers
Of a single match.
About to burn your thumb.
Knowing at any moment, it would have to be blown out.

And you knew, eventually,
The only light that would remain
Would be the light
You could see

When, in the pitch-black night
You closed your eyes

And remembered.

Light.

~ 21 ~

THE UNDEAD

January 6, 2021
They became rabid dogs
Foaming at the mouth
Fermenting
And fomenting
Their anger
Their fear
Their hatred
Their insecurity
Their white supremacy
Their stupidity
Their violence
Reminding us
Of our American origin story.
The brokenness that built this country
The hatred, the violence, the viciousness
They climbed the walls of the Capitol
With their MAGA hats and Trump flags
With their American Flags
And Blue Lives Matter flags
Their Confederate Flags
Their Swastikas.

Like cockroaches
They were climbing into every crevice
Coming out of everywhere
Just as they've been everywhere
For the past 4 years
For the past 245
The doctor
The teacher
Your neighbor
Your brother
Your uncle
They screamed nonsense
Filled with non-truths
Spit and foam flying from their forked tongues
And for four hours
We watched live on television
While they attempted to overthrow the US government
To find and murder our elected officials
To stop the process of a free and fair election
They showed up ready to bloody whoever stood in the way
And they did.
And
Yet,
Somehow,
They failed.

After months of seeing beatings on the street
Helicopters flying low
Tear gas, rubber bullets
Unprovoked attacks on protesters
We thought we understood something about
American fascism by now
But yet,

We sit.
Stunned.
For Hours.
On a Wednesday morning.

We watch in wonder at how this could happen.
How it cannot be stopped.
It's almost like
Our entire system
Was built to inherently
Protect
Them.
After watching months of protests
Against extrajudicial street murders
Met
With tear gas and batons
Riot gear and no mercy,
We now watch de-escalation techniques
Save lives
While the future of our Democracy
Hangs in the balance
While our country comes under attack.
Still, at the doors where it mattered most
The 'good cops' we hear about
They did their job.
They held the line.

We are all left
Questioning just how much violence and racism,
Just how much white supremacy and privilege,
Is part of our cultural inheritance,
And how can we give it back?
How do we excise this part of us?
It is too late?

Is this just always who we have been.
Will be.
Are.

Trying to live a beautiful life
Of freedom
Of good government
Of self-government
Among the undead,
Zombies,
A Violent faction,
Of the worst of us,
Who have always
And still,
Refuse to let us,

ALL
OF
US

Be free.

~ 22 ~

EPILOGUE

Saba's Story

The shadows have been growing for four years now.
I used to only see them at night time.
Small.
In the corner with the dirty laundry.
I ignored the shadow and the chores.
Then, the shadow grew.
It was there at dusk and at dawn.
And took over the room.

When I lost the first pregnancy, after 14 weeks loving my child,
I was still optimistic and told myself it would probably
just happen once.
I held my knees on the bathroom floor,
Knowing my husband couldn't heal a pain like this.
Knowing, his own grief kept him silent and still
In the other room.
Exactly where I didn't want him to be.

So, the shadow grew.
And sometimes the shadow stood between us

The mediator in our home
When we no longer had words to express
The depth of our sadness.
But, life has a funny way of moving on
Even while you're grieving
And the next thing you know, you're still living
And you're actually laughing sometimes.
Even though you laugh now with a hollow sound
Even you don't recognize,
A smile that doesn't reach your eyes.

And so it was in 2019, when I fell in love with my second child.
And this time, I was sick every morning
With each drop of bile at the back of my throat,
I smiled as I puked.
Grateful for this sign of life
They say that's a sign of a healthy baby.
Of lots of hormones coursing through your blood.
And this time was so different,
I was sure.

When we went to the doctor at the 8th week
They confirmed
That my morning sickness
And my baby
Were gone.

Morning sickness was now replaced
With the deepest, darkest
Grief.
The Shadow has weight now.
And depth.
The shadow now, holds all the dark
No light or laughter

Can pierce.

I would walk around surrounded by blackness
Like I'm blindfolded,
Looking for flashlights
But rejecting them when they are shone.
I just couldn't take the light any longer.
I resented it.
I hated it.
The shadow became a comfort - A friend.
The only thing I felt comfortable with.
Safe with.
The dark.

And then in Jan, 2020,
Our family was going to come for a visit.
I began preparing to get the shadow dry cleaned
Put it in the closet for safe keeping.
For weeks they would be with us,
Shining the light only family can shine
And the shadow,
This shadow that had become my friend
My blankie
A comfort I clung to as I avoided light
That dark comfort would have to stay put and away
While I enjoyed family and love and laughter and meals
But it's 2020,
Trump is the President of America
And I'm from Iran,
So first,
Threats of war.
Then, making good on the threats.

The flight our family could have been on

The flight so many families were on,
Canada bound,
Downed.
A government that shoots down its own passenger planes
Is no government at all.
The flights are all cancelled now.
There will be no trip this month.
They'll try again in March.

The shadow returns and now has a seat at the dinner table
Each night, watching television with us
While we take phone calls from our family in Iran
And our family here in Canada,
Who tell us of those 176 souls they knew,
That they loved
Now Gone. Ghosts. Grief.

G
L
O
B
A
L

P
A
N
D
E
M
I
C

Is declared on Friday the 13th,

March 13, 2020.
The shadow fills our whole house
Our entire block
Our entire city
Our entire hemisphere
The whole world
Is stuck inside the shadow now.
My husband and I make do as we trip over each other
In our work from home offices
In an apartment not meant for one work from home office,
Let alone two.
He still hasn't grieved like I need him to
So, we argue and fight and give each other dirty looks
But, the shadow is so present now,
All day,
Every day,
That at night
Is when it hides.
At night
Is when
The shadow's
Edges
Dim.
At night is when
The darkness, has a softer hue
Like maybe it's not black, but blue.

Like a night light
It burns away the pitch black now.
And then hides under the bed.
And after three months locked inside,
After 90 days with nobody, but each other
A softness returned.
A Desire

To light a fire.
To burn
And
This time,
There is a light
That stays.

A life that remains.
A life,
That brings,
Her own lantern.
She is now here
And she is now
The light.
Chasing the shadows away.

And now,
After death and endless dark
After pandemics and quarantines.
After being lost on dark and stormy seas.
There is a lighthouse.
Raya.
Farsi, for Light.

Because, the light was not in the wind
And the light was not in the earthquake
And the light was not in fire.

The light was always
In that

Still,
Small,
Voice.

ABOUT THE AUTHOR

T.M. Woodworth grew up in Omaha, Nebraska and is a proud alum of Benson High School, the University of Nebraska at Omaha where she studied journalism and organizational communication and Bellevue University where she earned her Bachelor's Degree in Business. She is a lifelong writer and story teller and some-time, slam poet. She is married, has two children and a fur baby. T.M. lived in Delta, BC for three years before returning to Omaha where she lives with her family. She loves scarves, boots, all the foods from all the places, binge watching Netflix, listening to 90's hip hop, acoustic chill and Taylor Swift. She loves to travel and imagine she's travelling.

This book is dedicated to those who lost their lives or loved ones, during the Covid pandemic and the healthcare workers who tirelessly, selflessly, tried to save as many lives as they could.

CPSIA information can be obtained
at www.ICGtesting.com
Printed in the USA
JSHW020021250223
38212JS00005B/84